Strawb Storm

written by Lucinda Cotter

illustrated by Anthea Whitworth

Raintree

Engage Literacy is published in 2013 by Raintree.
Raintree is an imprint of Capstone Global Library Limited, a company
incorporated in Engand and Wales having its registered office at 7 Pilgrim
Street, London, EC4V 6LB – Registered company number: 6695582
www.raintreepublishers.co.uk

Originally published in Australia by Hinkler Education, a division
of Hinkler Books Pty Ltd.
Text copyright © Lucinda Cotter 2012
Illustration copyright © Hinkler Books Pty Ltd 2012

Written by Lucinda Cotter
Lead authors Jay Dale and Anne Giulieri
Cover illustration and illustrations by Anthea Whitworth
Edited by Gwenda Smyth
UK edition edited by Dan Nunn, Catherine Veitch and Sian Smith
Designed by Susannah Low, Butterflyrocket Design

Strawberry Storm
ISBN: 978 1 406 26504 0
10 9 8 7 6 5 4 3 2 1

Printed and bound in China by Leo Paper Products Ltd

Contents

Chapter 1
A Job Well Done

It was Strawberry Saturday —
the day in spring when Misa
and Dad planted strawberries.
They worked together in the garden
all morning.
Dad dug over the rich, brown dirt
until it was soft and crumbly.
Misa made small holes with her spade
and carefully planted the strawberry plants.
Next, she watered each new plant.
Finally, she and Dad spread straw
around the plants like a cosy blanket.

"I think that's a job well done," said Dad,
as they put the tools away in the shed.

"I can't wait to eat the strawberries,"
said Misa.

"That won't be for another ten weeks
at least," laughed Dad.
"How about a ham sandwich, instead?"

Just then, Misa heard some thunder.
It made a rumbling sound.
She looked up at the sky.
"Dad!" she said. "Look at the clouds.
They're so big...and green!"

Chapter 2
A Storm
on the Way

"Uh-oh!" said Dad.
"There's a storm on the way.
A green sky can mean it's going
to hail, too."

"But what about the strawberry plants?"
asked Misa.
"Will they be okay?"

Dad shook his head.
"A hail storm is very bad
for strawberry plants.
They'll be cut to shreds."

As the first drops of rain began to fall,
Misa said to Dad,
"We have to do something to save
the strawberries.
We can't let them be shredded."

Dad scratched his head and thought.
"We need to cover the garden bed,"
he answered.
"The strawberries will be fine
if they are covered.
But what can we use?"

Misa looked up at the clouds.
The sky was getting darker and darker.
It reminded her of the time
she and Dad went camping.
There was a huge thunderstorm
and it rained non-stop.
They were stuck in their tent for two days.
That gave Misa an idea!

Chapter 3
Saving the Strawberries

"Dad!" cried Misa. "I've got an idea.
We could use our camping tent
to cover the strawberries!"

Dad smiled.
"What a clever girl you are," he said.
"The tent will be just right."

Dad quickly ran to the shed and came back
with a large bag.
He took everything out and unrolled the tent.

"We'll need a hammer," said Misa, running back to the shed.

"Good thinking," smiled Dad.

15

Dad hammered tent poles
into the strawberry bed.
When he was finished, Misa helped him
to spread the tent over the top of the poles.
Then Dad hammered tent pegs
into the ground.
"That should do it," said Dad.

Just then, there was a loud rumble
of thunder.
"The storm is nearly here," said Misa.
"I'll race you inside!"

Chapter 4
The Storm Hits

Misa stood at the kitchen window
looking out across the garden.
A flash of lightning lit up the clouds.
The rain was really coming down!
"At least the garden is having a good drink,"
smiled Misa.

RRRRRUMBLE!
BOOOOM!

The wind roared through the trees.
It made the branches bend and sway.

CRRRACK! BOOOOM!

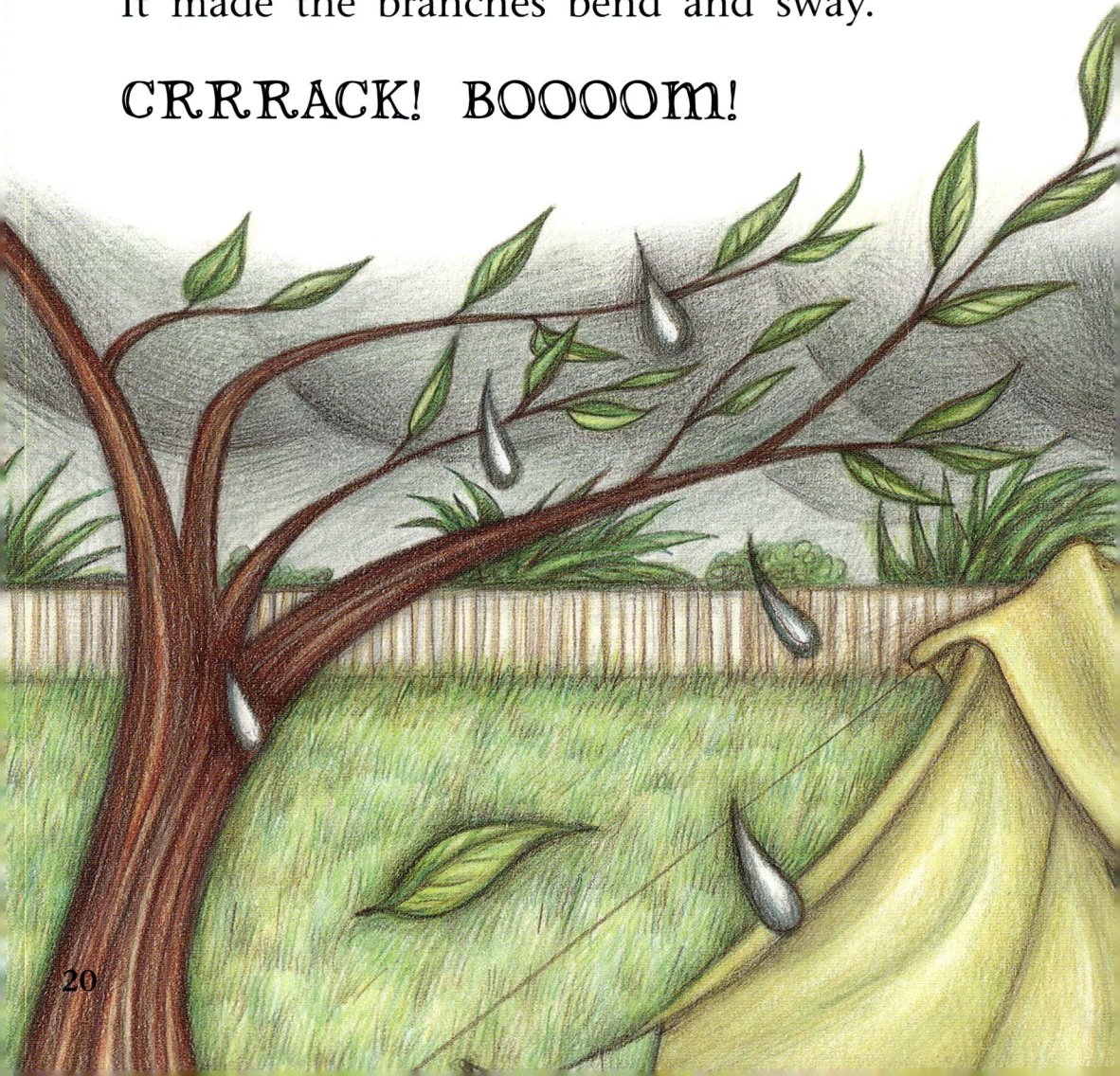

Misa jumped when the thunder
and lightning came.
The windows rattled and the lights
in the kitchen went off and on.

RAT-A-TAT-TAT-TAT-TAT!

Something was making a noise
on the tin roof.
When Misa looked out the window again,
she could not believe what she saw —
white balls were **bouncing** all over
the garden!
"Dad! It's hailing!" shouted Misa.
"It looks like snow!"
She pressed her nose against the window.
Lots of hailstones bounced off the tent
like ping-pong balls —
but the strawberry plants
were safe inside.

Ten weeks later, Misa made Dad
a special treat.
"Yum!" smiled Dad.
"Strawberries and ice-cream — my favourite!"

"They are our strawberries,"
said Misa, proudly.
"I call it Strawberry Storm!"